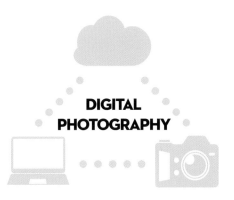

DIGITAL
PHOTOGRAPHY

PHOTOJOURNALISM

By John Hamilton

Abdo & Daughters
An imprint of Abdo Publishing | abdopublishing.com

abdopublishing.com

Published by Abdo Publishing, a division of ABDO, PO Box 398166, Minneapolis, Minnesota 55439. Copyright © 2019 by Abdo Consulting Group, Inc. International copyrights reserved in all countries. No part of this book may be reproduced in any form without written permission from the publisher. Abdo & Daughters™ is a trademark and logo of Abdo Publishing.

Printed in the United States of America, North Mankato, Minnesota.
082018
092018

THIS BOOK CONTAINS
RECYCLED MATERIALS

Editor: Sue Hamilton
Copy Editor: Bridget O'Brien
Graphic Design: Sue Hamilton
Cover Design: Candice Keimig and Pakou Moua
Cover Photos: John Hamilton & iStock
Interior Images: Alamy-pgs 4-5; AP-pgs 7 (bottom), 8 (bottom), 21 (top), 27, 32, 33 & 35 (right top); Canon USA-pg 17 (top inset); Des Moines Register/Mary Chind-pg 30; Eastman Kodak-pg 8 (top); Fujifilm North America-pg 13; Getty-pgs 6, 22, 23 (top), 29 (bottom), 31, 34 & 35 (left); iStock-pgs 11 (top), 14, 15, 16, 17 (top), 18, 19, 20 (top), 21 (bottom), 24, 26, 36 (middle), 38, 39, 40, 41, 42, 44 & 45 (top); John Hamilton-pgs 37 & 43; Minden-pg 35 (right bottom); NASA/Neil Armstrong-pg 7 (top); Nikon USA-pgs 9 (inset), 10, 14 (inset), 15 (inset), 16 (inset) & 20 (bottom); Shutterstock-pgs 9, 11 (bottom), 12, 17 (bottom), 23 (bottom), 25 & 36 (top, left, and right); The White House/Pete Souza-pg 28; U.S. Copyright Office-pg 45 (bottom); Zsolt Czegledi/EPA/Shutterstock-pg 29 (top).

Library of Congress Control Number: 2017963906
Publisher's Cataloging-in-Publication Data
Names: Hamilton, John, author.
Title: Photojournalism / by John Hamilton.
Description: Minneapolis, Minnesota : Abdo Publishing, 2019. | Series: Digital photography | Includes online resources and index.
Identifiers: ISBN 9781532115882 (lib.bdg.) | ISBN 9781532156816 (ebook)
Subjects: LCSH: Photojournalism--Juvenile literature. | News media--Juvenile literature. | News Photography--Juvenile literature. | Photography--Digital techniques--Juvenile literature.
Classification: DDC 778.22--dc23

CONTENTS

STORYTELLING WITH PICTURES

P hotojournalists bring us the news by showing us carefully crafted pictures. When something newsworthy occurs in the world today, we expect not only to be told what happened, but also to be shown. When astronauts go into space, or presidents win elections, or fighting breaks out in a war zone, we expect to see pictures. A photographer, somewhere, brings us those images.

Photojournalism isn't limited to news as it happens. It also shows us people and places we wouldn't normally see. It explains, in pictures, complicated issues. And it brings us closer to human emotion. Photojournalism tells us stories about science, sports, poverty, war, and all the other moments of our lives.

A photojournalist on assignment at a violent political street protest in Kathmandu, Nepal, in September 2005. The photographer's bright yellow vest identifies him as a member of the press.

THE MOST IMPORTANT TIP

The most important tip for capturing great moments is this: just be there. Sometimes, the best pictures are found where you least expect them. Always have your camera with you, no matter if it's a DSLR, a mirrorless camera, or even your cell phone.

Being where the news is happening, with your camera, is the single most important thing to being a good photojournalist. You don't need a college degree or years of training to take an important photograph of a newsworthy event.

A man uses his cell phone to capture an offshore waterspout as it develops.

LEFT: Buzz Aldrin, the second man to step on the Moon, is photographed by astronaut Neil Armstrong, July 1969.

BELOW: Tourist Carmen Taylor was on a ferry returning from the Statue of Liberty when she captured the jet that struck the World Trade Center's South Tower on September 11, 2001.

The pictures on this page are iconic. They are instantly recognizable as important news photographs. They have one thing in common: these photos were all taken by amateur photojournalists, with little or no training. The photographers happened to be in the right place at the right time, with their cameras ready.

Of course, if you do have training, know how to properly compose a photo, and thoroughly understand how to use your camera, you can create photographs with even more punch. Learning your craft will help you find where the news is happening, and better communicate its impact to your viewers. Knowing how to tell a story with your pictures is what good photojournalism is all about.

CAMERAS

Digital photography captures a scene when light passes through a lens and is focused onto an image sensor. The sensor converts the light into digital form. It is then stored as a file that can be transferred to a computer for later processing. The first portable digital camera was made by Eastman Kodak in 1975. It weighed eight pounds (3.6 kg) and shot only in black-and-white. Digital cameras as we know them today first became popular in the 1990s and early 2000s.

The first portable digital camera was made by Steven Sasson for Eastman Kodak in 1975.

Most photojournalism work today is done digitally because of the many advantages over film. One of the best parts is seeing your photos right away so you can change settings if needed. Also, you can take hundreds of shots on a single memory card. That reduces the chance of missing a great shot when you're busy changing a low-capacity film cartridge.

Photographers are sprayed by gas as police officers clash with striking workers during a demonstration in Paris, France.

With a DSLR (Digital Single Lens Reflex) camera, you can look through the viewfinder or use the camera's screen display to see exactly what you're shooting.

Most professional photojournalists today use DSLR (Digital Single Lens Reflex) cameras. With a DSLR, you actually peer through the camera lens so you can see exactly what you're shooting. Angle of view and sharpness are determined by the lens. DSLR lenses are "interchangeable," which means you can change one lens for another depending on your creative needs.

When light travels inside a DSLR, it is diverted by a mirror into a glass prism. It directs the light into the viewfinder. When you press the shutter release button, this "reflex" mirror flips up and the shutter behind it opens. Light strikes the image processor. After the exposure, the shutter closes, and the mirror flips back down.

The image sensor inside the camera has millions of light-capturing pixels that record an image. The greater the number of pixels, the higher the resolution of the picture. A 20-megapixel (20-million-pixel) sensor

The inside workings of a DSLR camera.

almost always has a better resolution than a 10-megapixel sensor. Modern DSLR sensors usually come equipped with at least 16 to 24 megapixels. The size of the image sensor is also important. The large sensors in many DSLRs produce the most detailed pictures, and they can capture images in low light without too much digital noise ruining the scene.

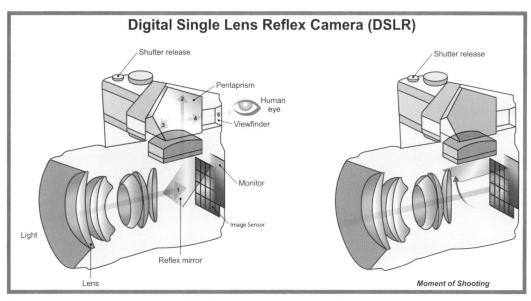

Digital Single Lens Reflex Camera (DSLR)

Shutter release
Pentaprism
Human eye
Viewfinder
Monitor
Image Sensor
Light
Reflex mirror
Lens

Shutter release

Moment of Shooting

This diagram shows how a DSLR camera creates a photograph.

8 TIPS **FOR CARING FOR YOUR** CAMERA

1. Use an air blower and microfiber cloth to clean your camera regularly.
2. Use a strap when carrying your camera.
3. When not in use, keep the camera safe in a bag or case.
4. Many photographers put a UV or skylight filter on the front of their lenses. These block ultraviolet rays from the Sun (which degrade image quality) and protect your expensive lenses from dust or scratches.
5. Make sure you always have spare batteries.
6. Keep your camera out of the rain.
7. Keep your camera out of hot cars.
8. Never leave your camera unattended.

Cell phones are commonly used as both a primary and backup camera. Most cell phones have a complicated lens arrangement. This has helped improve their photo quality greatly in recent years.

There is an old saying that the best camera is the one you have on you. For many people, that means a cell phone. The image quality of most cell phones has greatly improved in recent years. Most professional photographers carry one as a backup in case their DSLRs are not handy when a photo opportunity arises. Cell phones automatically focus and adjust exposure. Many allow you to manually override these settings for creative effects. Some even have dual lenses that let you simulate a shallow depth of field. This throws the background out of focus while keeping the subject sharp, which draws more attention to them.

Cell phone cameras do have disadvantages. It usually takes longer to set up and take a shot than with a DSLR. Adjusting exposure with an app and attaching a clip-on lens can be awkward. In fast-moving news situations, it's easier to miss a great shot with a cell phone. On the other hand, you'll always miss a shot if you don't carry some kind of camera.

Mirrorless cameras are becoming more popular each year. Like DSLRs, different lenses can be mounted on most of them (some have fixed lenses). However, there is no mirror or glass prism. This makes mirrorless cameras lightweight and quiet to shoot, which is a great advantage in many news situations. Most mirrorless cameras have excellent image quality, even in low light.

If you are a beginner, don't worry too much about which camera to buy. Think about what you want to do with it and which features are important to you. Amazing images can be taken with almost all digital cameras sold today. The truth is, it's the creative mind behind the camera that matters most.

A mirrorless camera produced by Fujifilm. This type of camera is lightweight and quiet to shoot, yet produces excellent image quality, even in low light.

LENSES

Just as important as your camera are the lenses you use. They determine the "field of view" of your scene. A wide-angle lens shows more of the surrounding area. A telephoto captures just a small part, which is why everything looks magnified.

A lens's field of view is measured in millimeters. A "normal" field of view captured by a full-frame image sensor is about 50mm. That is about the same as what you perceive with your eyes. Common wide-angle lenses are about 24mm to 35mm. Super-wide lenses start at about 10mm. Below that are fisheye lenses, which are used for special effects because of their distortion.

A fisheye lens causes distortion that bends straight lines, such as the horizon.

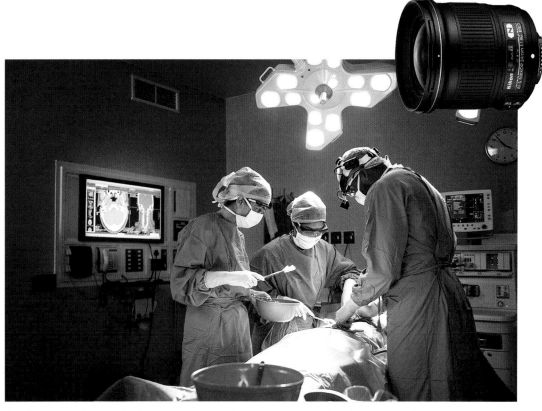
A 35mm wide-angle lens captures these surgeons in the operating room.

Most photojournalists own at least one wide-angle lens. (Wide-angle zooms are a popular choice.) These lenses make it easier to photograph large groups of people. They work well in low light. They also have a tremendous range of focus, or "depth of field." Foreground and background objects can both stay sharp if desired.

FILTERS

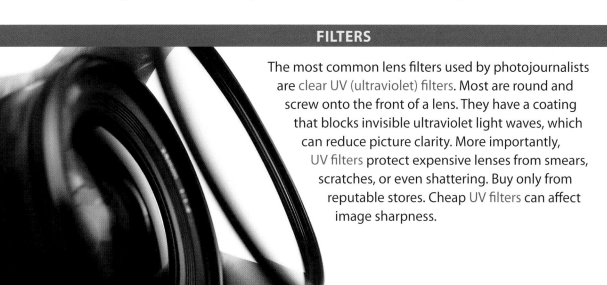

The most common lens filters used by photojournalists are clear UV (ultraviolet) filters. Most are round and screw onto the front of a lens. They have a coating that blocks invisible ultraviolet light waves, which can reduce picture clarity. More importantly, UV filters protect expensive lenses from smears, scratches, or even shattering. Buy only from reputable stores. Cheap UV filters can affect image sharpness.

A 200mm telephoto lens was used to capture this police training exercise.

The angle of view of a telephoto lens is very narrow. This is handy for cutting out the clutter around the edges of the scene you are photographing. Also, there will be many cases where you won't be able to physically get close to your subject, such as a fire or other kind of dangerous situation. A telephoto lens gives you extra "reach" when you are forced to shoot from a distance.

Telephotos start at around 85mm to 105mm. The most common telephoto zoom is about 80-200mm. These zooms are very versatile lenses that can be used in many situations, from sunsets to wildlife.

Above 200mm, telephoto lenses can be tricky to use, and very expensive. One solution is to use a teleconverter that attaches to your existing lenses. They can double the focal length with a small loss of quality, for a fraction of the cost.

A telephoto lens makes this Los Angeles traffic jam seem even more crowded.

Another added bonus of telephoto lenses is the "compression" effect they give. Because their angle of view is so narrow, people and things in the picture seem to be pressed close together, even if they're not in reality. This is a common trick to make crowds, cars, or other objects appear more congested than they really are.

LENS HOODS

Lens hoods are plastic (usually) extensions that fit onto the front of your lens. They keep Sun flare from washing out your photos. They can also protect your expensive lens's front glass element from bumps and scratches.

LENS HOOD

EXPOSURE

A camera's shutter-speed dial.

Exposure is the amount of light that strikes the camera's image sensor. Three settings determine the "correct" exposure. They include ISO, shutter speed, and aperture. All three work together.

ISO is the image sensor's sensitivity to light. If you double the ISO, you make the sensor twice as sensitive. However, more digital noise is then created. The lower the ISO, the better the quality. For example, when shooting in bright sunlight, you would normally set an ISO of 100 or 200. However, in dim scenes, you might increase it to 800. Otherwise, your exposures would be so long that you couldn't hold your camera steady enough to avoid blurring (camera shake). Blurring can also occur if your subject moves during long exposures.

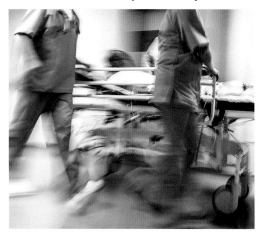

A slow shutter speed of 1/4 second causes moving objects to blur. This creates a sense of motion and urgency.

A fast shutter speed of 1/1,250 second freezes the swimmer, revealing details not normally seen by the human eye.

Choosing the right exposure is a balance between areas of light and dark (tone) and focus (depth of field). These are controlled by shutter speed and aperture.

Shutter speed is the length of time the camera's shutter opens to let light strike the image sensor. It is measured in seconds (usually a fraction of a second). Each setting is twice as long, or half as short, as the setting next to it. Shutter speeds must be fairly fast to avoid camera shake, usually in the range of 1/125 to 1/250 second. Wide-angle lenses can be used with slower shutter speeds.

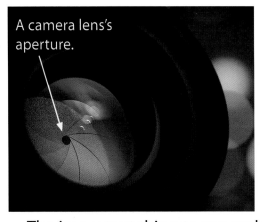
A camera lens's aperture.

Lenses have apertures, or holes, in the back where they are mounted to the camera. Apertures can be adjusted much like the irises in your eyes. They are measured in "f-stops." The smaller the f-stop number, the more light is allowed into the camera.

The important thing to remember is that if you increase one setting, such as shutter speed, then you must reduce the other setting (aperture) in order to get back to your original exposure.

When you are starting out, it's okay to put your camera on automatic. DSLRs have a setting on the exposure dial called "P," which stands for program mode. Modern cameras are like small computers. They examine the scene and figure out the math for you. The camera will pick a shutter speed and aperture combination. This will allow you to concentrate on other things, like focus and composition.

The exposure dial is set at "P" for program mode.

A wide aperture of f/4 created a shallow depth of field, isolating the subjects in this somber photo. The family is watching as a hearse carrying the body of a Minnesota corrections officer killed in the line of duty arrives at a cemetery.

As you get more practice taking pictures, you'll soon want to control these settings yourself in creative ways. For example, controlling the aperture also controls the amount of depth of field in your scene. That means you have control over what is in sharp focus.

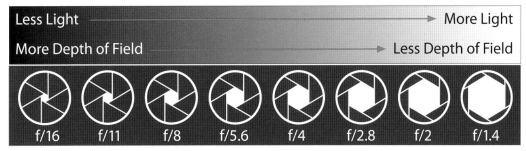

Typical lens f-stop settings.

GETTING A STEADY SHOT

It is important for photojournalists to document scenes with sharp, clear images. The best way to hold your camera steady is to tuck your elbows in near your body. The camera or telephoto lens should rest in the palm of your hand. Gently squeeze the shutter release. Don't stab at it with your finger.

Bulky tripods are not practical for most photojournalism work. News events change rapidly. Critical shots might be missed while fumbling with equipment. Also, it is easy for people to trip over tripod legs.

Without a steady camera support, however, there is the danger of camera shake. A photographer's hands tremble slightly while holding the camera, especially with a telephoto lens attached. These tiny movements happen several times per second. They cause scenes to appear jumpy in the viewfinder.

To properly handhold your camera, tuck your elbows in near your body and rest the camera in the palm of your hand.

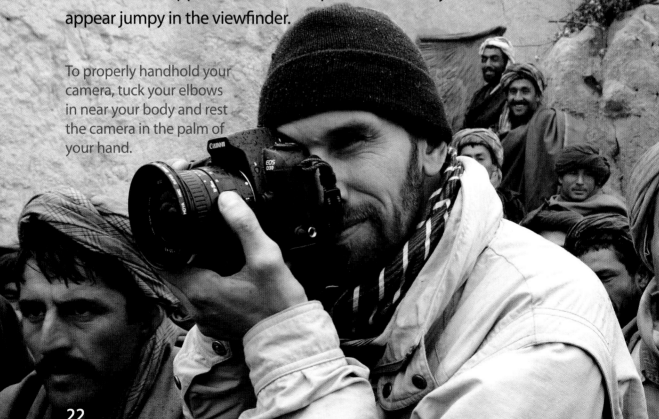

A steady hand and a fast shutter speed capture a Royal Air Force aerobatic team.

The camera shake effect gets worse as the focal length of the lens gets higher. It is much more difficult to handhold a 200mm lens than a 35mm lens. When the camera shutter opens, the shaky subject moves across the image sensor a tiny bit during the exposure. This is a common cause of blurry pictures. Camera shake might make the difference between taking a mere snapshot and capturing an image good enough to be published.

BEST SHUTTER SPEED FOR HANDHOLDING THE CAMERA

If you're handholding your camera, how do you know if the shutter speed is fast enough to create a sharp image? The rule of thumb is to shoot at a shutter speed higher than the reciprocal of the focal length of your lens. In other words, if you're shooting with a 200mm lens, you'll need a shutter speed of at least 1/200 second in order to get a sharp picture. If you're shooting with a wide-angle 24mm lens, you can go all the way down to 1/24 second. If you set your camera to "Program" or "Auto," it will calculate this for you.

Vibration reduction (VR), or image stabilization, is often activated by a switch on the lens barrel. This advanced technology often helps produce sharper images.

To combat camera shake, some lenses come with vibration reduction, also called image stabilization. The lenses contain motion-detecting sensors. Elements inside the lens move in the opposite direction of the motion. This cancels out much of the blurriness. Some cameras have vibration reduction built into their bodies. When shake is detected, the image sensor itself moves to cancel out the blur. This technology often makes it possible to shoot in dim lighting conditions.

RAISE YOUR ISO

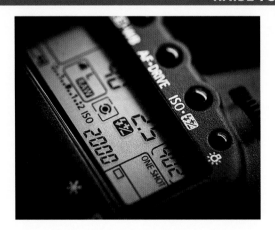

You're shooting with your lens wide open, perhaps at f/2.8. But your shutter speed is still too slow to capture action. Now what? Don't be afraid to raise your ISO, the image sensor's sensitivity to light. Crank it up, perhaps as high as ISO 1,600 or more, so that your shutter speed can sharply capture the action. You will see more digital noise in your photos, but that is better than missing the shot. Also, modern DSLRs work remarkably well, even at high ISOs.

A photojournalist uses a monopod to help steady and support his camera while shooting the Tour de France bicycle race.

Even though vibration-reduction lenses help tremendously, there are situations where photojournalists need physical support for their cameras. On very cloudy days, at night, or when shooting in badly lit meeting halls, there may not be enough light to successfully handhold a camera.

In these situations, many photojournalists use monopods. These metal or carbon fiber supports are a compromise between handholding a camera and using a bulky tripod. If you have to reposition yourself during a fast-paced news event, it is much easier to do so with a monopod attached. Also, monopods make it easier to access a second camera body, with a wider-angle lens, which you may have hanging around your neck as a backup for when action gets too close to shoot with a telephoto.

COMPOSITION

Composition is where creative photographers turn an ordinary image into a powerful statement. Photojournalists know that you don't need expensive equipment or exotic locations to make stunning images. Composition is all about arranging the scene in your viewfinder in the best way to tell your story.

Good composition uses many artistic elements. They include color, contrast, texture, framing, and natural lines. All of these things lead the viewer's eye to your subject. One of your most important goals is to reduce clutter in the scene. The best way to do that is to fill the frame with your subject. Be aware of empty space around your subject and get closer if you can.

Backgrounds can help or hurt your composition. Sometimes a busy background will give more meaning to your scene. Other times, it distracts from the person you're photographing. Before taking a photo, check to be sure things like poles or pillars don't seem to be growing out of the heads of your subjects. Large apertures, such as f/2.8 on many lenses, will blur the background, hiding much of the clutter.

THE RULE OF THIRDS

The "rule of thirds" is a way of dividing the viewfinder into sections and arranging your subject within the lines. Divide your viewfinder into three horizontal parts, and three vertical parts. Put your subject roughly near one of the intersecting lines. Don't always place your subjects in the center of the frame. Instead of a "rule," think of it as a helpful guideline. As you grow as a photographer, you will discover other ways to arrange elements in your frame that are interesting and tell a story.

THE DECISIVE MOMENT

O ne of the pioneers of photojournalism was French photographer Henri Cartier-Bresson (1908-2004). He was famous for capturing scenes he called "decisive moments." They are moments in time that are almost impossible to recreate, or candid facial expressions that are filled with honest emotion. Cartier-Bresson said that a photo taken a split second before or after the decisive moment pales in comparison to the impact of an image shot at just the right time.

White House photographer Pete Souza captures an iconic moment when Jacob Philadelphia touches President Obama's head to see if their hair feels the same.

A decisive moment is captured by photographer Zsolt Czegledi when a Swiss synchronized swimmer goes airborne during the 2017 FINA Swimming World Championships in Budapest, Hungary.

Decisive moments are often seen in sports photos, but they are everywhere. If you are patient and quietly observe people, you can find decisive moments in everyday life. You might see drama in simple scenes like people shopping for fruit at a street vendor, strangers arguing about politics, or even friends simply talking on a park bench.

It takes practice and good reflexes to capture the decisive moment. It also takes much patience. Observe a scene, plan your photograph, and wait for the right moment to reveal itself. It might not happen every time you shoot, but when you capture the decisive moment, you'll know you have a winning shot.

A light-hearted moment captured on a park bench.

ON ASSIGNMENT

SPOT NEWS

Spot news, also called breaking news, is reported as it happens, or shortly afterwards. It is of great interest to the public, and often involves destruction of property or harm to people. It is spot news when photojournalists take photos of burning buildings. Other examples include car accidents, severe weather, or violent protests.

If you happen to come across news as it happens, keep a safe distance. Be polite and show respect to police or any first responders at the scene, and do not cross police lines. Move if you are asked. If you happen to capture good pictures, your local newspapers or television stations might be interested in publishing them. Call or check their websites for submission guidelines.

Mary Chind's river rescue photograph won a 2010 Pulitzer Prize in Breaking News.

Photographer Andrew Holbrooke captured homeless men sleeping on top of a warm air vent in front of a wealthy display of fur coats in a New York store.

JUXTAPOSITION

Juxtaposition is when you photograph two things together that have a contrasting effect. In the viewer's mind, meaning is found because of the contrast. It is a good technique for showing differences in people or things, and making viewers wonder if those differences are good or bad.

Photojournalists can use juxtaposition to highlight problems in society. The technique is also used to point out issues that people seldom think about, or don't normally believe are connected.

An Olympic skier is frozen in time as she hurtles down the slopes.

SPORTS PHOTOGRAPHY

Some photojournalists specialize in sports. They have unique skills and professional equipment that helps them get the job done. Sports gear for photographers includes large telephoto lenses and cameras that can take good-quality photos even in the low light levels found in many stadiums.

Photojournalists who work for small newspapers and magazines may not have as much experience shooting sports. However, they will probably be given sports assignments, so they should know the basics. That includes knowing how to shoot with very fast shutter speeds to freeze action and using wide-open apertures such as f/2.8 to isolate athletes. The most important thing, however, is knowing the sport you shoot so you can anticipate when and where the peak action will occur.

A firefighter in full gear poses by a fire truck at the station.

ENVIRONMENTAL PORTRAITS

Photojournalists are often asked to take portraits of people when they're on assignment. The most common type is the environmental portrait. It is a good way to reveal someone's character with a single photograph.

Environmental portraits show people surrounded by items in their everyday life. These kinds of portraits show how people work, relax, and play. The key to shooting a good environmental portrait is to listen to your subjects. What gets them excited about their life and work? Your conversation will give you good clues to the kind of photo your subject wants. That, in turn, will help them relax, giving you a chance to take their picture with their guard down. That usually results in honest expressions that don't seem posed.

A firefighter's raw emotion during a funeral is captured by the camera.

HONEST EMOTION

Except for portraits, photos taken by photojournalists are not normally posed. Photojournalism's main job is to show viewers the news as it happens. That means people should act normally as if the camera is not there. Their expressions are not forced. Their emotions are honest and genuine.

When you shoot breaking news, it is easier to capture honest emotion. People are too occupied to worry about cameras recording them. With slower-moving news, how do you keep people from being self-conscious? Keep shooting, and don't intrude. People will soon ignore the camera and go about their business. When they drop their guard, capture their honest expressions.

The sizes of a tire, hailstone, and snake are clear when seen with scale objects.

SCALE

Showing scale in a photograph means showing how big or small something is compared to something else, usually an object well known to the viewer. Photojournalists use this technique to show the size of something unique and newsworthy, such as a large hailstone. If you shoot it by itself, the viewer really has no idea how big it is when viewed in print or on a screen. But if you shoot it next to a baseball, you can instantly tell that it came from a storm that must have been quite fierce. The human form is also a good measure of scale. An industrial tire might be big, but if you can see a small-looking person standing on top of it, you know that's one big tire indeed!

Research the area you are visiting and go out at dawn or dusk for beautiful light. Shoot not only from a distance, but also close-up, and at different angles.

TRAVEL PHOTOGRAPHY

When documenting life in another town or country, don't lug too much gear around. Carry a lightweight camera and one or two lenses. Some "do-it-all" zoom lenses have a very wide range. An 18-200mm zoom, which covers wide-angle to moderate telephoto, might be the only lens you need. By traveling light, you'll be able to do more exploring.

Research pays off. Find out in advance where the famous landmarks are. Shoot when the light is most beautiful, near dawn or dusk. Move around to get the best angles. Shoot small details and colorful backgrounds. Also, be sure to get people in your photos. Ask first, and be polite. You just might make new friends while you're at it.

To capture this scene at a high school talent show, the lens was opened wide at f/2.8, and the ISO raised to 1,600. Digital noise was reduced in Photoshop.

CONCERT PHOTOGRAPHY

To get good concert photos, you'll first need permission to shoot. At small venues such as high school talent contests, that shouldn't be a problem as long as you promise to stay out of the way and not use flash. Your biggest challenge will be low light levels. You'll need to open your lens up to its widest aperture, such as f/2.8. That will also give you a small depth of field, which helps separate the musicians from cluttered backgrounds.

Even with your lens wide open, you probably still won't have enough light to handhold your camera without risking blurry pictures. Raise your ISO until you have a fast shutter speed, at least 1/125 second. Post-processing software can help reduce the resulting digital noise.

DOCUMENTARY PHOTOGRAPHY

Sometimes, a single image isn't enough to tell a whole story. Photojournalists often use a series of images that work together. Documenting a story in this way helps viewers better understand a person or subject.

When choosing what to document, narrow your subject to give it more impact. For example, instead of doing a photo project on the environment, document the efforts of people to clean up a single park that is in their community. Follow them as often as you can, coming back for several days to capture their project in pictures.

There are many kinds of interesting events you can document. These include parades, county fairs, competitions, car shows, historical reenactments, or ethnic celebrations. Pick a subject that interests you, and then ask permission from the organizers to document it with your camera. Most groups will be grateful for the extra publicity.

Make sure the people you document aren't posing. Do not set up situations for the camera. Be a fly on the wall and observe what is happening. The people you photograph should act naturally, just as they would if you weren't there. They will soon get used to your presence and carry on with their activities.

Try *not* to have subjects pose in your photos.

This documentary photo series shows a group of people cleaning up a local park.

THE ETHICS OF PHOTOJOURNALISM

When people see photos coupled with news stories in newspapers, magazines, or websites, they expect them to be true to life. They expect the photos to be real, with no manipulation or enhancement that changes how the photographer saw the scene when the shutter button was pressed. Readers presume that the news they see is real. If they are betrayed, they may start believing that all news is fake, even photographs. Photojournalists, in order to keep their readers' trust, practice a system of ethics that guides their profession.

When editing photographs, professional photojournalists choose images that reflect the reality of the scene as they witnessed it. Ethical guidelines don't allow for photos to be radically altered. For example, in 2006 a photographer was dropped by a photo agency for cloning smoke and making it appear darker on an image of a burning building in Beirut, Lebanon, after an Israeli air strike. The photographer's unethical intent was to make the damage appear worse than it really was.

It is very easy to manipulate photos, especially with modern computer software such as Photoshop. Even before Photoshop, people have been manipulating photographs in advertisements and photo illustrations for decades. These photos all have a point of view, either to persuade or sell a product.

In photojournalism, the point is to inform or educate. Photos should not be manipulated or changed so much that they are no longer true to the story or event. Minor changes, of course, can be made, such as boosting contrast or correcting color casts. But the "truth" of the scene should be preserved as much as possible.

THE DIGITAL DARKROOM

Photos taken with modern cameras are usually well exposed and in focus, but there's always room for improvement. That's where the digital darkroom comes in. Fixing a photo's range of tones (its light and dark pixels) can improve it dramatically. Color balance, sharpening, and cropping are also common enhancements. These are all easy to perform with modern digital photo software, such as Photoshop, Lightroom, or GIMP. There are even inexpensive apps for cell phones that let you experiment with your photos.

Image editing software can be difficult to learn, but it is a fun way to improve your photos. Use the software's help menus, or search for online video instructions. Everyone was a beginner once, and many generous photographers are happy to share their skills.

Postproduction work can dramatically enhance a photo.

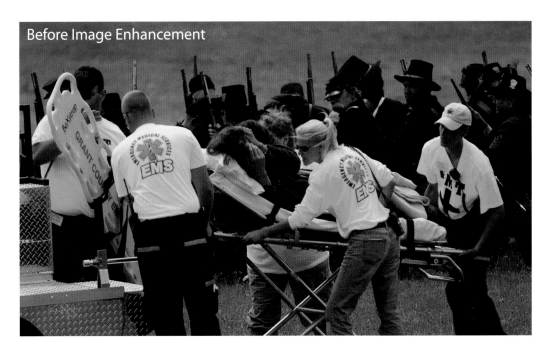

Before Image Enhancement

The photo above is before image enhancement. In Photoshop, the first task was to fix the exposure and contrast. Yellow was added to counter the blue cast, common on cloudy days. Color vibrance was boosted, and then a vignette circled the image to draw the viewer's eye toward the center of the frame.

After Image Enhancement

BACKING UP YOUR PHOTOS

Make copies of your digital images. Keep them safe on at least two storage devices. All hard drives will fail eventually. Without a backup, your photos will vanish, representing many months, perhaps years, of hard work.

In most professional studios, photos are backed up on several different devices. In addition to the hard drive on your main computer, use backup software every day to automatically copy all your photos onto a portable hard drive. These small devices get cheaper every year, with bigger capacities. Every few days or weeks, swap out the external drive with one that you might keep in a safe deposit box at your bank. This strategy is called having an off-site backup. If disaster strikes, such as your house burning down or washing away in a flood, your work will remain safe.

Portable hard drives hold a lot of photos and can be kept in different locations as off-site backups.

PORTABLE HARD DRIVE

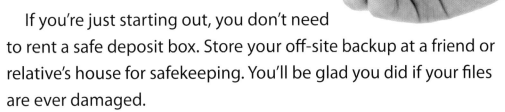

A USB flash drive is an easy and portable way to back up your photographs. It is a good device to use when traveling.

If you're just starting out, you don't need to rent a safe deposit box. Store your off-site backup at a friend or relative's house for safekeeping. You'll be glad you did if your files are ever damaged.

Some photographers store off-site backups in the Cloud. That means using the Internet to automatically store digital copies on large computer servers run by companies such as Dropbox, Apple, or Google. Cloud storage can be impractical because digital photo collections often grow to many gigabytes in size and could take days to upload. However, technology changes rapidly, and Cloud storage becomes more appealing with each passing year.

For extra protection, you can also keep your best files backed up on USB flash drives. After copying, toss them in a desk drawer. It's probably not totally necessary, but it'll give you peace of mind.

COPYRIGHT

Who owns your photos? You do, of course. The moment you press the shutter release button, you own the copyright to that image. To get even more protection, you can register your photos for a fee with the U.S. Copyright Office in Washington, DC, at copyright.gov. Registered or not, nobody has the right to use your images without your permission.

GLOSSARY

APERTURE
The opening in the lens that lets light pass through to the image sensor. The aperture is usually adjustable, and measured in f-stops.

CROPPING
Using image enhancement software in the digital darkroom to eliminate unwanted portions of an image, leaving only the most important part of the scene. Cropping is a powerful way to focus attention on your subject.

DEPTH OF FIELD
A range of distance (depth), from back to front, that is in sharp focus in your scene. A "shallow" depth of field has a very narrow range of sharp focus. It is seen most often with telephoto lenses when using large apertures (such as f/2.8), and is a useful technique for blurring distracting background clutter from your images.

DIGITAL NOISE
Noise is a collection of digital artifacts, which look like clumps of grains of sand that aren't really part of the scene. It occurs most often in low-light situations where the camera sensor is set with a high ISO number.

DIGITAL SINGLE LENS REFLEX (DSLR)
A digital single lens reflex camera is a kind of camera that features interchangeable lenses and sophisticated electronics. It captures images on a digital image sensor instead of film.

F-STOP
A number that is used to tell the size of a lens's opening, or aperture. Small numbers, such as f/2.8, represent a large aperture. Small apertures, which let in less light, include f/16 and f/22.

Image Sensor

The electronic device inside a digital camera that converts light into electronic signals, which are then processed and stored on a memory card.

ISO Number

A number that describes a camera sensor's sensitivity to light. Cameras that can shoot with high ISO numbers can capture images in very dim lighting conditions. The name ISO is the abbreviation for the International Organization for Standardization, a Swiss company. ISO is not an acronym for the company name. It is the root of the Greek word *isos*, which means "equal." It is pronounced "EYE-so."

Memory Card

After an image has been captured and processed by a digital camera, it is stored on a memory card, which is a solid-state storage device similar to a USB flash drive. Memory cards come in various speeds and storage capacities. Many can hold hundreds of images.

Sharpening

The human eye can detect contrast in a scene with amazing sharpness, but camera sensors are limited by the number of pixels they contain. This causes pictures to appear slightly blurry. Cameras and image editing software "sharpen" images to make them appear more in focus.

ONLINE RESOURCES

To learn more about photojournalism, visit abdobooklinks.com. These links are routinely monitored and updated to provide the most current information available.

INDEX